THE
PLEASURES
OF
ITALIAN
COOKING

The Pleasures of
Italian Cooking

BY ROMEO SALTA

WITH AN INTRODUCTION BY MYRA WALDO
PHOTOGRAPHS BY ROBERTO CARAMICO
ASSISTED BY JOHN CIOFALO

MACMILLAN PUBLISHING CO., INC.
NEW YORK

COLLIER MACMILLAN PUBLISHERS
LONDON

Macmillan Publishing Co., Inc.
866 Third Avenue, New York, N.Y. 10022
Collier Macmillan Canada, Ltd.

Printed in the United States of America

Contents

Author's Introduction

This is my cook book. It has taken me almost a lifetime to collect the recipes and I am very happy to share them with you now.

Brillat-Savarin once said: "It has been established that a succulent, delicate and careful diet delays the ravages of old age." Science tells us that wrinkles are caused by poorly-nourished skin and muscles that do not have the necessary resiliency. It seems only reasonable to conclude that women who eat properly will look younger than those who do not.

Italian food is extremely varied, and offers something different, indeed something unusual, every day of the year. The Italians have been wonderful cooks for many centuries, and in point of fact, it was an Italian woman who first won the coveted Cordon Bleu. It is an extremely interesting story, and one that always remains in my mind.

It seems that Louis XIV of France was very fond of a certain young Italian, the Duke of Nevers. The Duke was renowned as a great gourmet, and supervised the special court dinners. For his services, Louis awarded Nevers the Order of Saint-Espirit; this order was indicated by the wearing of a very wide blue ribbon (the Cordon Bleu). Dressed in this distinctive fashion, the Duke would proceed each morning to the market, in order to select personally the ingredients required for the King's table. Soon he became known in the market as "Monsieur Cordon Bleu." Louis even went to the trouble of personally selecting his wife, a niece of his current favorite, Madame de Montespan.

When the Duke died, his daughter took over his duties at the court, although it seems reasonable to suppose that the appointment was merely a kindly way of distracting the bereaved young woman, for she probably had little experience at the time. But it soon became apparent that the Duke's daughter was even more talented than her father, and the dinners and wines drew even greater praise. She married, and became the Duchess of Estrées, and the clamor arose for a suitable decoration for this unusually talented gourmet. She could not receive the Order of Saint-Esprit as it was reserved for men, and so the Order of the Cordon Bleu was especially created for her in honor of her skill and talent in the art of cooking.

And so, here are my recipes. Only a very few cooks are fortunate enough to win the Cordon Bleu, but all of us can prepare delicious dishes so that at least we can earn the title of Cordon Bleu among our family and friends.

Romeo Salta

Introduction

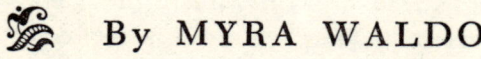 By MYRA WALDO

"Now art thou sociable
Now art thou Romeo;
Now art thou what thou art"
Shakespeare, *Romeo and Juliet: Act II, Scene iv*

ROMEO SALTA is a remarkable man.

Romeo, pronounced Ro-*may*-oh, was born in Italy, of course. He is one of twins, and his sister is named Juliet. Things like that can happen only in Italy.

His life has always been bound up with the sea. Romeo's father, a sailor in the Italian Royal Navy, was killed in 1910 during an explosion aboard that nation's first experimental submarine. A paternalistic Navy Department took care of the many little Saltalamacchia orphans, and helped them through the difficult years of adolescence. When a very young man, Romeo joined the Italian Navy and spent three years in the submarine service, following in his father's footsteps. I do not wish to say that Romeo was not a good sailor, but his officers certainly knew a talented cook when they saw one, for within a month after reporting for duty aboard a submarine, he was preparing meals for the officers and crew. When his naval service was concluded, the submarine officers tearfully asked Romeo to remain (they could even then visualize returning to the Italian equivalent of Spam), but he had other ideas. Romeo entered the merchant marine, and was soon assigned to a luxury liner, the *Conte Verde*, which then plied between Italian ports and the east coast of South America, including Rio de Janeiro, Santos and Buenos Aires. Aboard the *Conte Verde*, he was given the designation of *garzone di cucina*, which may sound somewhat grand, but which translates as "kitchen boy," or bus boy. It is one thing to be a first-class passenger aboard a luxury liner crossing the equator; it is another to be an overworked bus boy in an inside ship's kitchen, without ventilation, where the temperature was well over 100° morning, noon and night. One round trip through the tropics was enough, and he immediately transferred to the North Atlantic route, on board the *Conte Biancamano*. Romeo was promoted up the ladder, out of the kitchen and into the first-class dining room with the title of *piccolo*, or waiter's assistant. He looked forward with great anxiety to visting New York, for his two older brothers had already emigrated there. Romeo made precisely one trip, and the *Conte Biancamano* arrived in New York precisely two weeks before the 1929 stock market crash. But nothing could frighten our hero, and he remained in the United States, depression or not.

Romeo had to find work immediately, and at the age of twenty-four, he looked no more than seventeen. Also, finding that most Americans had some difficulty with his last name, he shortened it to Salta. His very first effort to obtain employment was successful. It was at the fabulous Central Park Casino, where he had to convince a skeptical *maître d'hôtel* that he actually had worked in the kitchen and dining room of transatlantic vessels, then regarded as the *sine qua non* of references for restaurant work. Romeo was employed as a waiter at the Central Park Casino for several years, then subsequently and in various capacities, at the Hotel Pierre, the Waldorf-Astoria and the St. Moritz. In 1933, he moved on to the Chicago World's Fair, working at the elaborate Century Club. When the Fair closed, Romeo decided to see what the western part of the United States was like, and he headed for California, landing ultimately in Hollywood. Romeo worked at all of the famous places in and around Los Angeles: the Clover Club, Vendôme and Trocadero. On his days off, Romeo wandered about the film capital and its environs looking for a good Italian meal, but all he could find were Italian-American restaurants featuring garish murals of the Bay of Naples, meat balls and spaghetti, and very loud jukeboxes. An authentic Italian meal could not be had in all of Southern California at any price, and Romeo determined to undertake what had always been his secret ambition—to open his own restaurant.

He was young, he had a little money saved, but not a great deal. Romeo found an old, atmospheric drugstore for sale, and remodeled the premises into a restaurant which he called the Chianti.

The Chianti was not an elaborate place, the decor was mediocre and there was sawdust on the floor, but the food was as good as Romeo could make it, and there was then, as now, no compromise with authenticity and quality. The very best food always costs money, and Romeo's prices were regarded as comparatively high, for only the finest was good enough for him. The going was quite rough at the beginning; in those days most Californians knew little or nothing about real Italian food, thinking of it in terms of an overly-spiced cuisine, loaded with garlic and tomato sauce. Of Italian wines, the residents of the West Coast knew even less, having been nurtured since childhood on the local products of Manischewitz and the Christian Brothers. Business was only fair, publicity just about nonexistent, and Romeo was beginning to wonder if life aboard ship would not be bearable, when a miraculous event occurred. A well-known newspaper columnist, Ed Sullivan, came in one evening with a large party of celebrities. A few days later, Ed Sullivan devoted an entire column to Romeo and the Chianti restaurant, heaping praise upon the owner and the food he served. From that moment on, Romeo and the Chianti restaurant were deluged with customers. Many celebrities of the movie capital made the Chianti restaurant their favorite, and soon Romeo became a celebrity in his own right.

After the war, with the advent of large-scale television, many of his customers began to move to New York, and they urged Romeo to do likewise. He did, and opened a new restaurant on West Fifty-sixth Street where he has remained ever since. Romeo regards it as the best move of his life, for he dearly loves New York. Unlike his experiences in getting started in California, no such problem was presented in New York, for his reputation and clientele had preceded him, and business was good from the beginning.

Personally, I have always had a strong liking for Italian food, particularly that of northern Italy, where the emphasis is upon cooking with butter (rather than oil), a moderate use of garlic (rather than the somewhat heavy hand of the southern part of Italy), and in general, a delicate and lighter fashion of preparing Italian food. As food consultant to Pan American Airways, I have traveled many times through all of Italy, including the cities and the hamlets, and have eaten in many hundreds of their restaurants. Back in New York, my heart would yearn for some northern Italian dishes, but although I tried every possible place, I could never find a truly good, northern Italian restaurant. Friends recommended me to one place or another, but the good restaurants were all southern-style (that is, in the fashion of Naples or Sicily), mostly on New York's Mulberry or Broome Streets. Finally, I ate at Romeo Salta's and I knew that I had found what I was looking for. Whenever my appetite calls for a *spaghettini alla carbonara,* or a *risotto alla Milanese,* or a luscious dessert like *torta mascherpone,* I head for Romeo's and know that I shall dine as well as in the best places in Italy. (If truth be told, often far better than in Italy.) In point of fact, and I do not say this lightly, Romeo's is one of the three or four best Italian restaurants in the world.

At the beginning, I said that Romeo Salta is a remarkable man. He *is* remarkable. Romeo still retains all of the qualities that brought him to the top in his chosen profession. He delights in meeting people, is naturally sociable; but even while he is engaged in the most engrossing conversation, his eagle eye is watching every employee, regarding every dish being served in his restaurant, and he never relaxes in the close, individual attention which marks the great restaurant and the great restaurant man.

The recipes in this book are authentic, uncompromisingly northern Italian, and best of all, easy to follow. There are all of the classic dishes of Florence, Milan, Genoa, Siena, Turin, Rome and Venice plus many of the delightful country-style preparations of the provinces. All in all, Romeo has brought together a superb collection of recipes.

I feel honored in being asked to write an introduction to this cookbook by Romeo Salta. It is a pleasure to do so, and to recommend to you both Romeo, the man, and his recipes.

Myra Waldo